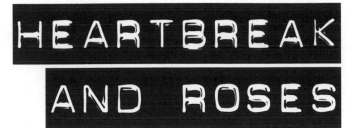

HEARTBREAK AND ROSES

Real Life Stories
of Troubled Love

by
Janet Bode
& Stan Mack

Delacorte Press / New York

Published by
Delacorte Press
Bantam Doubleday Dell Publishing Group, Inc.
1540 Broadway
New York, New York 10036

Book design by Claire Naylon Vaccaro

Text and illustrations copyright © 1994 by Janet Bode and Stan Mack

Library of Congress Cataloging in Publication Data

Bode, Janet.
    Heartbreak and roses : real life stories of troubled love / Janet Bode & Stan Mack.
        p.   cm.
    ISBN 0-385-32068-X
    1. Teenagers—United States—Sexual behavior—Juvenile literature.
    2. Interpersonal relations in adolescence—United States—Juvenile literature.
    3. Parent and teenager—United States—Juvenile literature. [1. Youth—Sexual behavior. 2. Interpersonal relations. 3. Parent and child. 4. Love.]
    I. Mack, Stanley. II. Title.
    HQ27.B616   1994
    306.7'0835—dc20   93-39012 CIP AC

Manufactured in the United States of America
August 1994
10 9 8 7 6 5 4 3 2 1

To
Rosemarie May Mazor

CONTENTS

THE COURSE OF TRUE LOVE

D o these love troubles sound familiar? Do you think that if only you had the right boyfriend or girlfriend, the rest of your life would take care of itself?

—Susan

I'm fifteen years old. For one year and two months I've been going out with Sean. Lately, I'm opening my eyes and seeing a jerk. He's guided by his ego and pride. He doesn't appreciate me, but he expects me to stick around.

I'm scared, though. He knows extremely personal things about me. If I break up with him, afterward he'll probably spread stories. I'm so confused.

—Jason

My life is going pretty well, except I'm lonely. I walk through the halls and see so many couples. All I need is to find a girl I want to be with. Doesn't sound so hard, huh? Still, it seems impossible. I guess I should just wait my turn. But the question is, how long?

—Chakira

I went out with this guy, Bobby, in October. Then we broke up, but I still love him. I think about him so much, it's getting me sick. My family could care less. They just say, "Chakira, are you ready to come out of your room now?"

4

I was going to a therapist until my stepmother refused to take me anymore. She wants me to move back with my mom. I can't trust my friends, especially about Bobby. They're back-stabbers. I have no one to talk to.

Susan, Jason, and Chakira put their feelings in letters. Other teenagers sat down and talked at length about what they were going through.

The result is this book of twelve short stories. Some tell of love gone wrong—violent love, obsessive love, tormented love leading to suicide attempts. Others speak of bittersweet love—battles for love fought against outside forces.

As in life, and especially life in the teen years, the course of love in these stories is turbulent. They may upset you. They may comfort you. They may also help you see your own love problems more clearly.

Two of the stories are told with words and pictures. The emotions, though, are just the same as the others. Think of them as videos in book form.

Scattered through the pages are fact boxes. Each contains a brief newspaper account that relates to teen dating. These, too, may give you a little more insight into your own love life.

But the main goal here is to provide you with a collection of compelling stories. Open the door of your imagination, and read them the way you'd read a book of fiction.

Then at times stop. Remind yourself, these are the words of real teenagers. To protect their identities, the names have been changed and a few details altered, but the tales they recount are all true.

The students come from different ethnic and economic backgrounds. Some attend inner-city public schools. Others go to suburban and small-town junior and senior high schools. One of the storytellers could even be sitting next to you in your first-period class.

HEARTBREAK AND ROSES

(Bonnie)

For nine months after Michael and I broke up, I didn't want to talk to a guy on the phone. I didn't want a guy to put his arm around me. I didn't want to go near another guy.

My friends were, like, "You know, Bonnie, all guys aren't the same."

But Michael changed my life.

He made me scared of guys, scared that someday they're going to change, too. The way he did.

Now I've been going out with Vince for about two months. He's nice to me. Still, I think, "What if we get into a fight or something? Is he going to hit me?"

I can't help it. I get nervous. Every time I'm with Vince, I get flashbacks of Michael. Michael would pressure me into sex.

The one time Vince and I tried to have sex, it was totally different from Michael. Still, I "saw" Michael hitting me. I said, "I have to stop."

"That's okay," Vince said.

Vince asked me, "What happened with Michael?"

I told him. I moved here from Michigan to live with my mom. I didn't have many friends, but this one girl, Jacklynn, went to a church that was having a teen weekend. A whole bunch of kids would get together and spend the night at the church.

That's where I met Michael. The first thing I noticed was he was cute. Honestly I can say I started staring at him. He had a girlfriend, but he kept looking back at me.

When the weekend was over, I went to Jacklynn's to search through her yearbook. There he was. We were both going into eighth grade.

You know how guys like girls who are new in school. There were guys who liked me. But there was something about Michael that I liked more. We started going out and stuff.

HIS ALONE

Six months go by, and everything is fine. We are together every day. We don't fight. The most he does is get mad if another guy looks at me.

One day he says, "Bonnie, to tell you the truth, my first intention was to use you."

"What's that supposed to mean?" I ask him.

"All my friends wanted to go out with you. I wanted to be, 'Well, I *have* her.' But I've ended up falling in love with you."

Then we have sex. We are each other's first. He starts getting more possessive.

It's so gradual, piece by piece; I don't really notice. When I do, I tell myself, "Michael's doing it because he loves me so much." I tell him, "Sometimes I want to hang out with my girlfriends."

He's, like, "They're losers. Anyway, they talk behind your back."

"I want a social life. I want to have my own friends."

"I want you all to myself," he says. "I sleep with your picture."

Meanwhile, he's out cheating behind my back. My mom and I are shopping, and I see him walking down the street holding hands with some girl. I start crying. He's always saying, "I could get other girls easy if I wasn't going out with you."

Instead of yelling at him, I yell at the girls.

When Michael and I have sex, he never uses anything. He says, "I don't feel like it, and you can't make me." The time I think I might be pregnant, he says, "Just tell your mom you got raped."

When I yell at him for that, he apologizes.

I'll tell you what, I prayed that night, "God, please don't let me be pregnant." I did the whole rosary. The next morning, I got my period. I said, "Thank you, God."

CONTROL

Michael told me what to wear and what not to wear. If I wore something he didn't approve of, he would make me put on his sweatshirt. My mom bought me an outfit for my birthday. The shirt was a little short. Michael said, "Wear a tank top under it."

I told him, "No."

I wore it to school the way I liked it, and when he saw me, he started screaming, "You slut," in front of everybody.

"Get out of this relationship," I told myself. I don't know why, but I just couldn't do it. After each fight, Michael would bring me a dozen roses.

I start marking in my diary the days that Michael hits me. It gets to be once or twice a week. I leave my diary out, figuring, you know how moms are. She'll probably read it.

If she does, we never really talk about it.

Instead I make up answers. When she asks about my latest bruise, I tell her, "Oh, I fell off the couch." I tell myself the same old thing: "Bonnie, this relationship is no good for you."

For that whole year, I can't get out. I guess I like him too much.

He shows up at my house with some of his friends. My mom says I can't have guys in if she's not here.

Michael knows that. When I won't let him in, he starts hitting the door until it breaks.

He charges in, throwing things, saying, "I'm going to kill you." He picks up the phone and begins to call more of his friends to come by. When I try to stop him, he hits me over the head with the receiver.

I black out and come to.

"Get out!" I scream. I call his dad and say, "Can you come over and pick up your son?"

By the time his dad gets here, everyone's gone. He doesn't believe me about what happened.

Later that day, Michael is on the phone to me. He says, "I'm sorry. I don't know what came over me." The next day, he stops by when my mom is at work. He hands me a dozen roses, and he leaves.

Everything is fine again, I think.

THREATS

For the last six months of our relationship, we'd break up at *least* once a week. Anything you could think of, he'd fight about. Like, my mom didn't want me talking on the phone after nine o'clock.

He'd call whenever he felt like it. If the line was busy, he'd do an emergency breakthrough. Then he'd scream, "You better be around to talk to me when I want you!"

One night my mom finally took the phone off the hook. We didn't know that my grandma was trying to get ahold of us to say that my mother's brother had died.

Of course, I was upset. I called Michael the next day, saying my uncle died and they couldn't get through 'cause the phone was busy.

"Who cares," he said.

I was devastated.

That was it! I told him, "We're over."

He said, "You break up with me, I'm going to kill myself."

I didn't believe him.

The next day, he called up and said, "I just slit my wrist." I ran all the way to his house. Hysterical. I opened his door. He was lying there on the floor with a towel around his hand.

I said, "Oh, no, please say you didn't." I pulled the towel off his hand and—nothing.

"You lied to me!"

He said, "Now that I have you, I'm not going to let you go." There was nobody else at his house.

I said, "Please, just let me go on with my life."

"No, Bonnie," he said, "you are my life."

I was scared.

I tried to get past him and out the front door. He

grabbed me. He slapped me across the face. He got me in a choke hold. I started crying.

Then he started crying.

He said, "Bonnie, I love you. I didn't mean to do that. I'm *so* sorry."

"I can't take it," I said. "I want out."

"You want out of here?" he said. "Fine. Fine." He pushed me off the top step of the front porch.

I started walking home, and then I realized, "Well, he said he loved me. Maybe he just needs me."

I thought maybe I wasn't good enough for him.

I imagined following him everywhere, begging him, "Please, forgive me. I'll do everything you want."

Why did I want him back?

Why did I feel it was my fault?

Why did I feel I was nothing without him?

I don't know. What I know is he was my first love. Maybe I drove him to it by breaking up with him.

He called me and called me. When I finally gave in and called him back, he screamed, "What do you want!" at the top of his lungs.

DEPROGRAMMING MYSELF

That day it just clicks into me: Michael doesn't think about anybody but himself. There are plenty of guys out there. I shouldn't be abused. I'm only fourteen years old.

I tell him over the phone, "We have to break up."

"No other guy will love you as much as I do," he says.

The more I think about him and our relationship, the more upset I am. I look at my diary again and again. I'm used to having him around. I think about getting back together.

I stay in my room the whole weekend. I make myself remember each time he's hit me. Each time he's screamed at me. Each time he's pressured me to have sex. Each time I've heard he's cheating on me. Each time I can't do something because of him.

I have to, like, deprogram myself to fall out of love with him.

I start trying to make friends. When I begin to tell Jacklynn some of the details, she cries with me.

I try to put Michael out of my mind as much as I can.

I keep myself occupied.

I talk to my mom.

When I want to call him, I call someone else.

I write in my diary about my feelings.

I go run around the track at school until I can hardly walk.

I make dinner.

I listen to other people's problems.

I pray to God to help me be strong.

PICTURE PERFECT

It's been nearly a year since Michael. Sometimes I feel he's on my shoulder when Vince and I are together.

He's saying, "Bonnie, how could you do this? You know I still love you."

I say to myself, "Don't think about him."

Vince thinks it's no big deal that I hang out with my friends. He likes them, too. We all spend time together.

I have my first job. My mom leaves me a note in the morning. She says, "Dear Bonnie, I want to see my little girl on her first day at work. Please have Vince take your picture."

I tell him, "Don't bother. I look stupid in this outfit I have to wear."

Vince says, "You look cute! You always do."

I smile and say, "Okay, go ahead and take my picture."

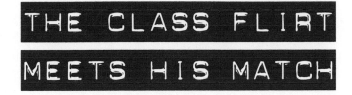

THE CLASS FLIRT
MEETS HIS MATCH

(Louis)

My last year at middle school, I was voted class flirt. I was the sweet-talker, the wanderer. I'd never settle down. One night a week, the guys and I had a condom run. We'd buy different kinds and trade them.

I like hanging out with the guys. I really like girls, too. For some reason I can talk to them. I can cry, too. I have no idea why. Girls *love* it, though. It's the way guys should be.

One night that summer before tenth grade, I was at the carnival with a bunch of buddies. When I saw this girl, I said to my friend Tom, "She is so hot."

"She'll never give you the time of day," he said.

"We'll see about that," I told him.

She was playing this game where you throw a softball at a target. I'd won it, like, twelve times. She was on her third ball. I knew she was going to miss.

I ran up to her and said, "You're doing it all wrong! Stand over here. It's my lucky spot."

"Why don't you do it?" she said.

"No, you can."

She threw the ball, and she won!

I said, "Well, since you won, I have to give you my phone number." She smiled and took it. Her name, she told me, was Maura.

The next day, I was at her front door. She had a boyfriend but was in the process of breaking up with him. I asked her out.

It never occurred to me she might be a world-class flirt herself.

KISSING MAURA

When I meet Maura, she's thirteen. I'm sixteen. She tells me she's fourteen, going to be fifteen. Much later I ask her, "How come you lied to me?"

She goes, "Would you really have stood there and talked to a thirteen-year-old?"

Back in the very beginning, she says, "What would be the perfect girl for you?"

" 'Cause I'm a player, no girl has ever trusted me. For a girl to look me in the eye and tell me that she actually trusts me—*wow*."

"Louis," she says, "I trust you."

From then on, for me everything revolves around Maura. I'm spending all my money and my time on her until my mom says, "I thought you were saving for a car?"

I say, "Yeah, I'll save." I put a couple bucks away, and then I end up blowing it. I buy Maura presents. I take her out to dinner, to the movies, to the beach.

Two o'clock in the morning when I leave work, I detour to her house. I knock on her window to tell her sweet dreams and kiss her good night.

Let me tell you, I can spend hours just kissing Maura. I let my tongue caress every part of her lips. I kiss the top one, the bottom one, then trace along them to the corners where they meet. I'm always gentle with her. With my touch I tell her how I feel.

OBSESSION

There are dances at her middle school. I say, "Go ahead."

She says, "Only if you're out in the parking lot waiting for me." So I'm out there, acting like a jerk, waiting for her. First they just kick me off the property. Then I get trespassing cards. Next I'm almost arrested.

My buddy Tom says, "Come on, Louis, let's go shoot some baskets." I think about it for two seconds until Maura comes by. I leave my friends.

They try not to get mad at me, but I start hearing from them, "You're ditching us, and for a younger girl."

Maura and I get into trouble because we never do anything with our families anymore, either. My mom's worried. She thinks we're spending too much time together. I tell her, "You don't know what you're talking about."

Her mom says, "Don't you hang out with anyone else?"

My mom starts in on the pregnancy lectures. "Maura's a little girl. Don't forget that. If she gets pregnant, you're in *deep* trouble."

I say, "Don't worry!"

"I'm your mother," she says. "I'm supposed to worry."

Her dad starts being pretty rude. He's, like, "Louis is three years older, and he's too perfect." I guess he thinks the nicer a guy is, the further he'll get with his daughter.

EXPLORATION

If he only knew. When it came to sex and stuff, Maura was pushy. She was the virgin. I wasn't. She started asking me when we would do it.

I said, "You don't have to do that." I thought that she might have felt obligated to do something because she was younger with an older guy.

She kept bringing it up. "Well, what does it feel like?" she'd ask.

"Come on," I said. "I'm not a girl. I can't tell you that much."

She was hanging out with older girls, the wild dressers. I didn't know what they talked about behind closed doors, but they filled up her head with the message: Do it!

Don't get me wrong. I thought sex was great. But there were times when not having sex could be great in its own way.

Like, we were in my room, lying on my bed. I was on the bottom, Maura on top. We were kissing and kissing, and after a while my hands started exploring. I touched her hair, her neck, her shoulders, her back.

I ran my fingers over her clothes, over her skin. I brushed my cheeks and my lips along her arms and those thighs of hers. She had these tiny, golden hairs on her legs that kind of teased me. The ache I felt for her made it better.

See, before all this my mom and I had been close. She *knows* what's going on. She's the one who talks to me about sex and all that. Not so much my dad. He only jokes about it. Instead of condom, he says, "Don't forget your umbrella."

My mom says, "Guys can be pressured, too. Listen to your best judgment, not your hormones. When you're ready, you'll know. Maura may think she's ready, but afterward she could regret it."

POSSESSION

One night after we'd been going out for almost three months, Maura goes, "I really want to do it."

I say, "You'll chicken out."

Then she says, "Do you have condoms?"

I tell her, "I'm not stupid. I'm always prepared."

The next day when she comes over, she finds my condoms. I have this rule. If a girl and I are about to have sex, I will never open up a condom.

I think for a guy to do that makes it look like he wants it too much. Then if he opens it and the girl says no, the guy gets mad at her.

We're fooling around and Maura opens a condom. I'm thinking, "Ohmigod."

She says, "You know this is my first time."

From then on, it gets out of hand. We have sex a couple times a week. I'm scared she'll get pregnant. She doesn't seem to care.

One day she says, "Should we stop using condoms?"

I'm thinking, "Everybody's always saying it feels better without it." And I'm sure it does. When I think of my future, I see a wife and two kids. Maura, of course, is the wife.

I get a wonderful feeling at the thought of being the father of her children. We'd make new lives—together —and I'd love them as much as I love their mother.

That's in the future. This is now.

"No," I tell her. "For now we can't make love without a condom."

She's glad I wear it. It proves to her how much I care

about her. I'd never do anything to hurt her. I feel like there's nothing else in my life, just her.

RUMORS

At a New Year's Eve party, Maura noticed this guy Richard. He was flirting with her. Was she coming on to him?

Richard! The kid across the street. I grew up with him. I taught him everything. He's a smooth talker. He's younger than me and in her school. He would see her more than me during the school day. I felt like a dummy.

It's hard to trust your friends when it comes to a girl. There are more guys who'll stab their friends over that. Even if the guy says no, if the girl is good-looking, really sweet and cherry, it's what every guy wants.

Four and a half months into our relationship, Maura's feelings were turning toward him. I started worrying, "I'm going to lose you."

She was, like, "No, you won't."

The worrying turned into arguing. I said, "You're going to end up with Richard."

"No, I'm not!"

"*Yes, you are!*"

Everything was going downhill.

Maura said, "Why don't you go look at the girls in high school?"

"But I love you," I told her.

Every day I heard a new rumor. Richard screwed her over. She was with this guy Adam. I didn't believe what anybody told me. I had too much trust in her. She wouldn't break up with me.

It was tearing me apart.

I felt that we had something good going and we were throwing it away for nothing. I call her up and say, "I know you want to break up with me. Why don't you do it?"

She says, "I still love you."

I think, "If she loves me, can she care about Richard?" I say, "Well, who is it? Me? Richard? Adam? Some other guy altogether?"

"You," she says.

I go, "Why are you lying to me?" We start to really argue then, and finally I say, "It's over!" She starts crying.

After it's officially over, we stay on the phone for another four hours. I even warn her how certain guys are when it comes to sex. "Some are out for one thing. They figure if you've lost your virginity, they can go do it with you."

By the end of the conversation, it's like nothing ever happened. We're back together.

Then two days later, she's going out with some other

kid! Her friends are telling me, "You know, Louis, she is a flirt."

One of them says, "She told me she's using the guy to get over you."

I was going crazy.

TRAPPED IN LOVE

Maura called. She felt it'd be better if she gave me back my chain and stuff. I went over to her house.

Along with the chain, she handed me a poem she started the night before. It was called "Trapped in Love." She said she was stuck on the last sentence.

I tell her, "Don't finish it. I will."

I wanted to write how I felt right then. How it didn't matter what we talked about. How I just wanted to follow her with my eyes. How I wanted time to stop to keep the memory fresh.

Was I loving her so much that it made her feel trapped?

By then we both were crying. She says, "I still love you."

When she kisses me, I say, "You can't do that. I'm trying to get over you."

She says, "Why did we mess up? You're the only guy who never hurt me."

The phone rang. She went to answer it. From the other room I could hear her talking. She said some guy's name. She laughed at something he must have said.

I recognized her voice. It was the voice I thought she saved only for me. She was sweet-talking this guy. She was flirting with him.

I went home in shock.

REENTRY

I know now that a girlfriend or boyfriend is just that. They are not life. You don't have to be with them twenty-four hours a day, seven days a week. You have other friends, too.

Even when you love the person, she's still a friend, which means she can hang out with your other friends. They're bound to have something in common. If they don't, you should wonder, is there a problem?

In the months I was with Maura, I'll never know how much I missed out on. My friends would say, "Yeah, man, we went to this party. You missed the fun."

You should listen to your family. You ignore them, they're going to ignore you. And you need them.

Once Tom and my other friends found out we'd broken up for good, they did call. They didn't remind me

too often that I was a jerk to forget about everybody for
Maura. And then look how she treated me, they'd add.

SELF-PROTECTION

Maura's been calling. She leaves messages. She says,
"You're never home. All I get is your answering ma-
chine. How come you don't call me?"

One day she catches me in. I go, "Yeah, I get your
messages."

"Louis," she says, "I can't live without you. And I
know you can't live without me."

I get mad that she says that. I'm, like, "Wait a second. I'm seeing a girl right now. I'm living without you,
aren't I?"

Still, she knows she's right. I only say that to protect
myself.

F∆CT B⊙X

For Some, Youthful Courting Has Become a Game of Abuse

A nationwide survey of high school and junior high students released in June 1993 found that a high number of girls and boys said they had been groped and subjected to sexually explicit put-downs in school hallways. According to the study, more than two thirds of girls and forty-two percent of boys reported being touched, grabbed, or pinched on school grounds.

Some young people admit they can be confused about where to draw the line between flirting and harassment, advances and abuse, media images and reality, and right and wrong.
—Melinda Henneberger with Michel Marriott, *The New York Times*, July 11, 1993

NAKED ALONE
TOGETHER

(Pam)

I 'm not the kind of girl who can't go two days without a boyfriend. And I'm not searching for some guy because I haven't seen my father since I was five living in Utah.

Still, I do have an ideal guy in mind. I want him to be responsible. That's important. In the looks department he's Brian Bosworth. He's Donald Trump's money, Albert Einstein's brains, James Dean's sensitivity. And he treats me good.

Last year there I was, waiting for the right guy to come along. With everybody always talking about how *great* sex was, it was hard to wait, but I was trying. I told myself being friends was a lot better than being lovers.

Then starting a few months ago, I began to think my whole world was falling apart. First, my friend Betsy moved to Florida. Next, Emily's boyfriend wouldn't stop beating her up.

Worst of all, Kelly got killed. I understood death comes to everyone, but not to fifteen-year-old girls with plans and dreams.

I stayed in my room and talked on the phone to my last good girlfriend, Tina. We told each other all our problems. She wrote poems for her pain, and my pain, too. She always gave me copies.

Tina wrote one for Emily about her rotten boyfriend. She called it "Black and Blue."

When I showed it to my mom, she said, "Pam, go out. Make some more friends."

BACKSEAT LOVE

I paint my fingernails black. I put on a striped T-shirt, my cut-offs, and black leather Keds with hot pink tongues and laces. I'm ready to head for P&B— Pocket and Billiards.

Right away I'm meeting all these people—Graham, Ronny, Alan, Maria. Some are from school. Some are older. Maria's an emancipated minor; she doesn't live with any parent. Afterward, we go to her apartment to party.

What I do is spend the night there. I tell my mom I'm staying at Maria's. She says, "Fine, be home by eleven tomorrow morning." Mom has no idea what happens once I'm out our door.

I don't tell her that within a month I lose my virginity to Graham, one of those Cool Guys. On a Saturday morning he shows up at Maria's and says, "Want a ride home?"

"Sure," I say.

We go driving around until he pulls into an elementary school parking lot. He says, "Let's be friends forever. Make love to me."

Maybe it's the emotional buildup. Curiosity. Timing. Mainly I'm thinking, Graham's not gonna like me unless I do it. "Yeah," I tell him, and we climb into the back seat of his Geo-Metro.

I don't tell him I'm a virgin. Even if I did, I don't

know if it would make any difference. I'm thinking, "Sex is going to be, like, real nice," stuff like that. Instead, I'm moaning not from pleasure, from pain. There's even blood!

How can people keep doing it all the time, saying it's so fun, when it hurts like hell? At least this first time. I guess it's different for somebody who's losing her virginity to a guy she *really* loves, not someone she just thinks she sort of cares about.

Fifteen minutes later, we're back in the front seat heading for my home. If you want to know the truth, I'm embarrassed about where it happened.

I try not to think about Graham. I can tell we're only going to be see-ya-in-class friends. I'm right. Within two weeks we don't talk on the phone or go out or anything.

THE STERILE STORY

I've been told that you have to be honest with your feelings. I think I'm too open too quickly. I trust too much. Right away, everyone knows my strengths and my weaknesses. Ronny did.

Later I hear that Ronny calls himself the gigolo of P&B. The night I meet him, he's complaining that Irene, his ex, played him out through their whole relationship.

He says, "I told her that I didn't want to have anything to do with her."

I listen. I know Irene from school. We've been friends. I don't know what to think.

He starts pressuring me. Lots of guys, when they're pressuring you, say, "Oh, I'm sterile." Ronny's not the one who told me, Maria did. That's how I know it's true that he's sterile.

I don't think of asking him about protection. I don't think of STDs. I don't know how to say no. I just go ahead. The next day alone in my room, I read Tina's poem, "Naked Alone Together." She wrote it for me.

STD SCARE

My mom yells, "Irene's on the phone!"

"Not this past weekend, but the week before, I got chlamydia from Ronny," Irene says.

I hang up, scared. Why is she telling me this? Should I believe her? I know for a fact she slept with Graham, then Trippet before she slept with Ronny, then who knows who else. Maybe she got it from Trippet and gave it to Ronny?

I go to the county department of health for a checkup. They tell me I don't have chlamydia, but I do have an infection. It could be that Ronny cut my vagina wall and something about bacteria from my period.

All I hear is I don't have chlamydia. I take the condoms they give me and leave.

PROMISE ME

Maria tells her boyfriend's best friend, Peter, to come over after P&B. I had told her I wanted to meet him. So he did, and we sat around, and one thing led to another. I don't have to tell you what.

"You have a perfect body," Peter says to me. He likes that my hair's natural, not Kelly Bundy blond.

I sleep with him once, twice, three times. We talk about almost anything. He's real smart. He's working at Houlihan's to save money for college.

When I tell Tina about him, she writes "Hollow Promises."

I think of those words when Peter tells me, "We can't sleep together anymore."

"What?" I say.

"What you have going against you is your age."

"What's wrong with my age?"

He goes, "My age."

Peter's twenty, and I'm fifteen. Of course I told my mom he's seventeen. On my way home I keep wishing

I'd said something dramatic like, "Well, Peter, I still offer you my shoulder and my ear. I'll give you my opinion when you ask for it, my silence when you don't." But I didn't.

THREE GUYS TOO MANY

By the time I'm home, I break down. I try to make sense out of what I'm going through. Okay, I've slept with three different guys.

But everybody who hangs out at P&B has sex with each other at one time or another. Yet hardly anybody is even going out together, like boyfriend-girlfriend.

I don't think we should do that anymore. After you sleep with someone, you should be close. You should stay true.

I make a decision. I won't go out with guys purely for sex. I'll go out with them to see if they understand me or not. So far, it seems one guy's like the next. Maybe I'll just try to cover up my emotions.

My mom hears me crying and comes in my room. I tell her some of this stuff about my friends. I don't let her know I've been sexually active. "Maybe you're spending too much time caring about other people and not enough time caring about yourself," she says.

She gives me a hug.

I want my mom to meet someone who really loves her and she can really love. I know she wants to get married again. She'd like to share our split level in suburbia.

That's what I'd like for both of us: Mom married and me in a steady relationship. But until that happens, at least I have a good mom and my sweet friend, Tina.

F⅄CT B⦿X

Sex and the Teenage Girl:
More Partners, More Risks

For all the warnings about AIDS, American teenagers are taking more sexual partners than ever—and more risks for sexually transmitted diseases.

A study released last week revealed that 62 percent of sexually active girls aged 15 to 19 had had two or more sexual partners. In a 1971 survey, 39 percent had had at least two partners.

Of sexually active women under 20, 30 percent had had four or more sexual partners, and 5 percent reported having had 10 or more partners.

The study suggested that the earlier sexual activity was initiated, the faster a girl moved on to her second partner.

—Tamar Lewin, *The New York Times*,
December 13, 1992

DECLARATION OF INDEPENDENCE

(Ofelia)

W hen I was a kid, I thought one day Prince Charming would come into my life. We'd fall madly in love. All my problems would go away. We'd live happily ever after. Sure. I woke up. I stopped looking. Prince who?

I didn't think about Antoine that way. He just happened.

I had known him a long time. We talked together. I don't remember why, but we began calling each other, too. Finally he said, "Enough of this playing around. Do you like me?"

I said, "I'd like to get to know you better."

That was the start. I wanted to make sure I had strong feelings for him; it wasn't just my physical emotions taking over.

After a while I decided I did have feelings. I wasn't in love with the idea of love. I knew it was a big responsibility to have a relationship that included sex. Still, I was seventeen. I was ready to be with Antoine.

Once I made that decision, it was hard to keep it to myself. I thought, "How am I going to go about actually having sex with him? Do I sneak away? Do I tell my mom?"

My mom barely tolerated him. She kept hoping he'd disappear from the picture. Antoine comes from a poor family. He's used to being out in the street.

I've always had a sheltered life. My family's very protective. Whatever I need, I get. I don't know what it's like to be out at all hours of the morning. That's exciting to me.

What my mom sees is that Antoine's black. What I see is an outgoing, good-looking guy. You want to be around him. He's not the kind to fall into the locker-room trap. You know, the boys who talk about how they scored.

On the other side, Antoine's family is prejudiced against white people. He admits they're not happy about my skin color, and that's just part of the problem.

Antoine is able-bodied. I think of myself as differently abled. For ten years I've been partially paralyzed and had nerve problems because of an automobile accident. I use a wheelchair.

Antoine's family is always asking him, "Why would you want to take the responsibility? For a girl like that?"

He tells them, "It doesn't bother me." He grew up around people in wheelchairs. It's not a mystery for him. Until this year I feared rejection. I was self-conscious about my body to begin with.

I worried, "Well, maybe the chair will be such a turn-off, he'll never see past it." But Antoine saw me, the person, and not the chair. Anyway, I have a pretty great personality.

LOVE PLANS

Privacy is a problem for us. Antoine's family lives in an apartment building on the tenth floor. The elevator is usually broken. I live in a two-story house with my mom, my two sisters, my aunt, my uncle, and three cousins. My father died when I was an infant.

I can't do a lot of intimate things for myself. I need home attendants to help me. None of them stays too long. There are always different people doing different things for me.

My mom has power over me, more than most teen-agers have to cope with. She can be intimidating. When I was little, I idolized her. Now I know she's human.

Antoine and I started planning how we could be together. We decided, first things first: What are the different kinds of contraception, and which ones are best for us? With my disability, what are my limitations on how my hands work?

I went to Planned Parenthood. I told the counselor, "My boyfriend and I are thinking about using condoms and the foam."

"Will you be able to manipulate the spermicide ap-plicator?" the counselor asked.

"No," I said. "I can't use my hands enough to put in a diaphragm or push the foam applicator. It's okay, though. My boyfriend says he'll do it."

She said, "Good for you two. Some young women

would never dream of asking their partner to put in the diaphragm."

I couldn't believe it. I said, "You mean girls are going to do something so personal and intimate with a guy, but they can't talk about contraception with him?"

"Surprising, huh?" the counselor said.

Of course, Planned Parenthood was easy compared to telling my mother. I remember that conversation like it was yesterday. What came out was, "Mom, Antoine wants to be with me."

Her eyes became slits. She's thinking, "Here this black guy is coming. He's going to take my baby away." I'm embarrassed to even be talking to my mom about this stuff.

I'm thinking, "I could have phrased it better."

"I knew this was going to come up," she says. "Ofelia, at least wait till school's over."

I agree. I want to wait, anyway.

COMPLETELY ALONE

I always thought the first time I make love, it will be so romantic. For us, it's more like a schoolbook comedy.

We're now ready to figure out where we can do it: a hotel. We look through the Yellow Pages to call places to compare the price. After we pick a hotel, Antoine says, "It's not close to public transportation. How should we get there?"

"We could rent a van," I say. We call an ambulette service to see how much that would cost. We can afford it, so we say, "Okay."

I'm packing a bag when the phone rings and the ambulette people say, "The van broke down. Can we send a car?"

We don't know what to do. Because of my paralysis, I can't sit up well without support. Antoine says, "I have to learn to put you in and out of a car. I'll start with this." I don't know how much I weigh, but I'm no light-weight.

I'm falling for Antoine more each day.

The driver gets here, and he only speaks Spanish. I speak some Spanish, but I don't know how to get to the hotel. Just as we're calling another car, my mom comes home!

She knows where we're going. And she doesn't want to be here to see us actually drive away. She leaves. I feel awful.

I'm not nervous—until we get there. I look back at it now and realize the hotel was a dump. But that day Antoine puts me at ease.

We get in the room, and all I can see is the *bed*.

My heart starts beating.

Antoine turns on the TV.

We're completely alone.

That has never happened before. Someone is always in and out of my house. The instant he starts putting me in the bed, it flashes through my mind, *"I don't want to be here."* I don't say anything.

Antoine is good. He doesn't push me. Still, sex is not wonderful. Since I can't walk, the hymen never stretches. His penis inside me really hurts. Afterward I'm, like, that's it? I try to hide from Antoine that it takes so long before the hurt goes away.

He asks me, "How was it? Tell the truth."

"Well, it was not what I expected," I say.

We leave on a Friday afternoon and come back Sunday. We walk in the door, and there's my mother. I keep thinking that she's thinking about Antoine and me together. I can't look at her. This is the woman who gave birth to me and raised me, and she doesn't approve.

TEARS, TISSUES, AND TOMORROW

Antoine and I have been together two years now. Sometimes it's hard to say whether a boyfriend's worth it. I've been through a lot. Because I never have much privacy, we have to sneak around to be together. That takes its toll.

Antoine recently had a child by an ex-girlfriend. If it

had been some girl he just met, that would be different. But it was someone he'd loved. I was devastated. I felt it was my fault.

I went to the point where I didn't want to deal with life anymore. I thought about suicide, and more than once. Instead, I found a counselor to talk to. She spent many tissues on me. Even when I didn't want to talk, she got me to.

It took a while to accept the child. Sometimes my sad feelings are still there.

I see the baby. Antoine brings it over. I don't cry as much as I used to, though. You know why? For all the pain with Antoine, he's also helped me realize there are things I can handle on my own.

He's always encouraged me to explore my neighborhood. I remember the first time I went to the park by myself. It's four blocks away. I was scared, but it felt good. I told some friends, and they were shocked I went by myself.

They said, "It's not safe."

I said, "It's not safe for anybody."

Before Antoine, I would never have dreamed about having my own apartment. I was terrified of being alone. I was *so* dependent on my mother. Now I form my own opinions. I'm getting anxious to move out. I've applied to a place, only I haven't told my mom yet.

I'd like Antoine to be in my future. It's shaky right

now. He comes to see me practically every day. He says, "It bothers me that you won't tell your mother you're not happy with the way things are."

When he says that, I get angry with myself. Now, though, it's a healthier anger. I direct my anger in positive ways. I went by a store that was being remodeled. It's three floors and has no elevator. Who's going to carry me and my chair up the stairs?

I ask the manager, and he says, "Oh, we're going to put in an elevator soon."

I went back, and there still wasn't one. I think, "Should I make a case about it?" I'd like to be an activist, and partly I have Antoine to thank for that.

Maybe he's a 1990s Prince Charming. Antoine has helped me figure out who I am and what my beliefs are. He's helped me explore my feelings and begin to be independent. And he's helped me be just like any other teenager.

LOVE ON THE RUN

(Kirsten)

58

A WOMAN FOUND ME AND TOOK ME TO THE HOSPITAL. I WAS BLEEDING REAL BAD. THEY SAID I LOST THE BABY.

THEN MY MOM AND DAD WERE, LIKE, "WE'RE SORRY, KIRSTEN." BUT I HAD HATE IN ME.

TOO LATE TO BE SORRY.

UNDERCOVER LOVE

(Seth)

I live in a laid-back suburb of New York City. My parents are politically liberal and morally conservative. They're raising me on marriage, children, and family. They're very strict.

It's clear they don't want me growing up too fast. And in this quiet town, they're afraid of what might be going on after midnight, from drugs to violence to running with the wrong crowd.

But I have a different problem. I just didn't realize it until this year.

To get me away from their fears, the summer before tenth grade, they sent me to a Mediterranean sailing camp. That's where I met my first girlfriend, Heather.

She was a cool blonde who wore New Wave clothes, my ideal at the time. I was terrified she wouldn't think I was good enough for her. I was naïve. Heather was aggressive. We did a lot of things, but I didn't want to have sex.

I was embarrassed to be naked in front of someone. I didn't feel ugly; I felt awkward. What Heather and I did was always under the covers.

By the time I got home, though, I knew I wanted a social life. I didn't want to be popular. I just wanted to be with the people in my class who looked like they were having a good time.

Every step of the way has become a battle. The first time I asked to go to a party, my parents wanted to drive me there and pick me up at ten o'clock, my curfew!

I'd do anything to get out. Lie. Sneak. Pretend things. They started putting on more restrictions. They wanted to know every move I was making. I began to stay over at friends'.

We were into drinking, drugs, and trips to the city. We became regulars at one club in particular and would get passes to come back each time we went. I'd leave home in jeans and a T-shirt. In my bag I had my club gear ready to go.

The one night I came home smelling of alcohol, my mother said, "Seth, you're going to a therapist."

The therapist said, "Do you have a drinking problem?"

I said, "Well, I go out on Friday night and have four or five beers. Is that a problem?"

"No," he said.

I didn't tell him I was starting to fall in love with a guy. It happened before I knew it.

SEPTEMBER—NOVEMBER

We've been friends for a couple years. This year we have a lot of classes together. We go to the same parties.

If you ask me what I like about him, I'd say, everything. He seems secure in his life. I'm in constant turmoil. We have the same interests. We even dress similarly.

He's good-looking. Other people like him a lot. His name is Zach, and he's on my mind all the time. I wonder, "Why is this happening?"

I'm angry. I don't want to be gay. And more than anything, I don't want anybody to know. Not Zach, either. I pray he doesn't feel the same way. I don't know what's going to happen if he does.

The idea of a gay relationship upsets me, depresses me. I spend hours in my room doing nothing but listening to why-does-God-hate-me music. My life is a mistake.

I don't look in the phone directory for a gay hotline or support group. I don't want to deal with it. I want these feelings to go away.

One afternoon, I do some research in the library. I look up *homosexuality* in an encyclopedia. Most of what I read is technical. I want to know, can I do anything to change my feelings?

I'm afraid the only cure I'll read about is some therapist zapping a gay man with a cattle prod while showing him pictures of men together.

Are people born gay, or is it in the raising? I read both arguments. A girl I know comes up and says, "Hey, what are you reading?" I hide the page.

There are about six hundred students in our high

school. To be openly gay isn't tolerated. You'd be targets of the jocks and the kind who throw bottles at the school on weekends. You could be in physical danger.

One night after I've been at a school play, some guys corner me. They push me around. They call me faggot. They don't know—it's just an expression. But it scares me.

A girl I know stands around laughing. She seems to enjoy seeing me get in trouble. Teens are cruel to begin with. I had negative feelings about gays, too.

My parents say, "As long as gays stay in Greenwich Village and don't bother anybody, they can do what they want. Well, almost anything. We don't want to see them on the street having a parade. And we don't want to see them teaching our kids in school."

All I know about gays is they are supposed to be into casual sex. That's opposite of how I feel. All I want is to be so emotionally attached that eventually we sleep together.

I go into the city by myself, and somebody's put a tremendous sign in front of Grand Central Station: AIDS IS THE WRATH OF GOD ON ALL HOMOSEXUALS. ALL HOMOSEXUALS MUST DIE.

Some days at school, I don't think I'm going to make it through. I feel I'm falling off the edge. On weekends I get up at four in the afternoon.

It's harder and harder to pretend I just think of Zach as a friend. We spend time together, and when I leave, I'm barely out the door before I'm crying about it.

I can't keep it inside anymore. A bunch of us are at a party. We're stoned. I say to my friend Wendy, "There's something I want to tell you, but I'm afraid it might change how you think of me."

"You can trust me," she says.

"I'm attracted to Zach."

"Seth, it's obvious."

"Do you think he might be gay?" I ask her.

"I'm pretty sure he's not. I'm not saying you shouldn't be gay. But your attraction to Zach is not going to work. It's just trouble for you."

Wendy has had lots of relationships. She knows how these things work. She says, "Give yourself time. You won't feel as bad as you do right now."

I don't believe her. I do feel relief, though. I've spoken the words: *I'm attracted to Zach.*

"If you keep sitting in your room, mulling over it, crying, it's going to get worse," she says. "Find someone else."

Telling Wendy starts a chain reaction. Another

friend, Andrea, overheard our conversation. She says, "Zach's been wondering what's going on. You have to talk to him. If you ignore it, you're going to ruin your friendship."

I run the idea of sex with a man through my head. I'm affectionate. But I don't know how to get beyond that. Even with Zach, the fantasy isn't about great sex. I want to be with him. I want to have a sharing, caring relationship.

I'm depressed.

MARCH–MAY

Zach and I are at a party. I get drunk. We leave together, but we're going in opposite directions. Before we say good-bye, I tell him, "I'm sorry to do this, but there's something I need to talk to you about."

I have spent hours figuring out how to tell him. I'm prepared for his answer. I see two possibilities: He feels the same way. Or he's horrified.

I'm frightened.

I don't think he'll be nasty. But saying anything to him could hurt our friendship. What if he *does* feel the same? I don't understand anything about being gay.

Finally I say it: "Zach, I'm attracted to you."

He answers right away. "Oh, that's okay," he says. "It doesn't bother me."

It doesn't bother him! What's that supposed to mean? He likes me? He hates me? He wants to be anywhere but having this conversation? Is he surprised? Will this change our friendship?

Is he telling the truth?

I can't believe it. I didn't anticipate that answer. It leaves too many doors open. I can't bring myself to say, "Well, do you think you're gay? Even if you are, you aren't attracted to me?"

I go through this whole buildup, and I get an ambiguous answer. I'm almost angry. For the million things I want to say, all I can manage is "I'm sorry."

"There's nothing to be sorry about," Zach says. And then we say good night.

I'm so late coming home, my mother's waiting for me. She starts to search me. She's suspicious of drugs. My father comes downstairs and is lecturing me on being rude to my mother, when she finds my cigarettes.

They're furious. To them, smoking is a dirty habit. Only someone who hates himself smokes. I run past them to my room. I'm sure they're thinking, "What a troubled young man." It's always my troubles. They never see that they're involved.

I want them to go to family counseling. My father refuses, and my mother sends me instead. I'm sixteen years old and already on my second therapist.

This one isn't any better than the first one. There I am with a bearded, forty-five-year-old man who smokes a pipe. He's going to listen to my sexual problems? He talks about the different stages of a child and asks about my sexual fantasies.

JUNE–SEPTEMBER

After that conversation, Zach pretends it never happened. I'm convinced he hates me. Still, I feel a little better because my feelings are no longer a complete secret. The obsession, though, is worse. To relieve the tension, I get stoned on the way to school and again coming home. My life seems hopeless.

I'm so unhappy day-to-day, I try to believe there will be some sort of justice in the future. Nobody should go through this for no reason.

My parents send me to Atlanta for the summer to stay with my aunt and uncle. I still have not touched a guy. I haven't done much more with a girl.

Within a couple weeks of going to Georgia, I meet this girl, Stephanie. We become friends. One afternoon, she bleaches my hair. We get drunk and have sex.

Emotionally I'm glad to get that over with. But I realize I'm not cut out to have relationships like that with a girl. We decide not to do that anymore.

I don't know if she puts two and two together, but that same day she introduces me to Josh.

Josh and I go out and then come back to his home. Everybody is gone. I kind of let sex happen. I'm curious. I need someone to push the issue, to say, "Let's try this."

Afterward, I go back to my aunt and uncle's and take a two-hour shower. Until now I haven't really dealt with being gay. My experience with Josh tells me I not only have to accept my homosexuality, I have to accept what gay sex is: the actual physical contact and what it means.

I'm tired of being angry at myself. Instead, I want to be honest. I tell myself, "Even if I can't tell other people the truth about me, I have to make sure I know what the truth is. The fact is, for now, to survive, I have to be pretty closeted."

But that makes me angry all over again. I wish I could tell straight teenagers: Don't judge other people. Gay and lesbian teens are no worse and no better than you are.

You may fear us. You may hate us. But don't turn those into action: Don't beat us. Don't persecute us. Don't take the time to worry about us. If nothing else, leave us alone.

It's easy to say, "No one close to me is homosexual." Well, do you really know what goes on in everyone's heart?

After vacation I know I have to convince myself and

Zach that my feelings for him aren't serious anymore. I want to talk to him. Keep the friendship going.

Maybe we can talk about how we had so much in common. I saw a lot in him I wanted to be. I'll bring it up that way. I'll never use the word *love*. I'll never say why I felt the way I did.

"Don't worry," I'll say. "It was a supercrush, and it's over."

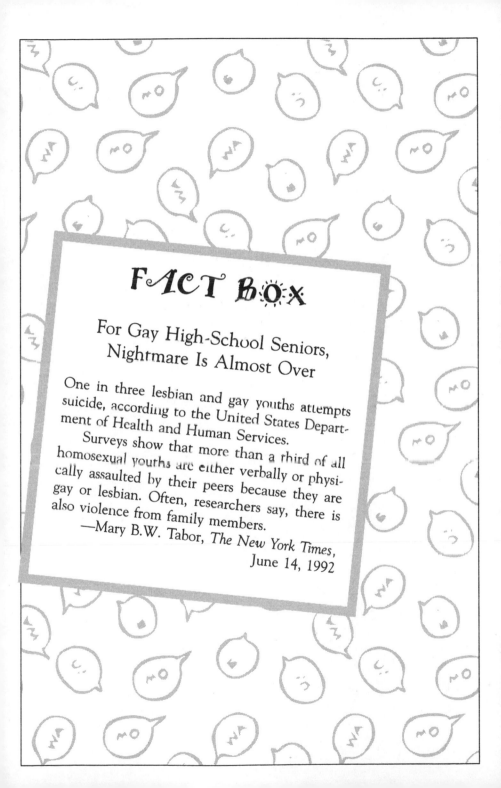

F∕ICT B⦂O⦂X

For Gay High-School Seniors, Nightmare Is Almost Over

One in three lesbian and gay youths attempts suicide, according to the United States Department of Health and Human Services.

Surveys show that more than a third of all homosexual youths are either verbally or physically assaulted by their peers because they are gay or lesbian. Often, researchers say, there is also violence from family members.

—Mary B.W. Tabor, *The New York Times,*
June 14, 1992

A NIGHTMARE OF A
DREAM GUY

(Charlene)

H is name is Forrest. He's sixteen. I'm fourteen. And with me, it's nearly love at first sight. We're both living with our families in a homeless shelter. It isn't terrible the way most of them are.

This one is an enormous house. I live upstairs in a two-bedroom apartment. Forrest is downstairs in a three-bedroom place. There's a hospital up the street and stores along the way. It's a good neighborhood.

Right after we move in, I'm playing *Monopoly* with Amanda and Bronwyn, two of his sisters. Amanda says, "You know, Forrest likes you."

I'm, like, "Really?"

She just smiles.

"Well, why doesn't he come and talk to me?"

So he does.

He says he's walking over to the deli. "I'll come along," I tell him.

He doesn't remind me of anybody I've ever known. He isn't fat and he isn't skinny. He is *built*. He has a masculine face, hard and handsome.

That first time we talk, I couldn't tell you what we said. But I could feel this something inside of me. Something I'd been looking for. It's hard to explain. I still don't understand why I had those feelings.

On the way home from the deli, Forrest and I go behind a church, and he kisses me. The kiss is unbelievable. My head starts spinning. May 13—I'll never forget that day.

I knew I wanted to be with him. I didn't know what a whole big-deal situation it was going to be.

SWEET LOVE

At first our parents didn't know about us. His sisters kept it all quiet. We tried hard to find some privacy. There was a park about a half-mile away. We walked there to be alone.

We'd kissed. Lay in the grass. He'd push me on the swings. With him I didn't have to pretend. I could be myself.

Most guys are so centered around themselves that they don't even care about their girlfriends. Not Forrest. It wasn't all about himself. It was about me and him.

He was loving. My little brother was like his son. My sister was his own sister. That's how much he cared about them.

He wrote me notes. I'd read them on the bus on the way to school. He would tell me how much he loved me. How much he wanted to marry me. How many kids he wanted us to have. All those good things.

I used to think that the guy I would love would love me for who I am. He'd be sentimental and have *passion* for me. Passion not in a lustful way but in a way that showed he wanted to uphold me. He'd praise me for the good things I did, make me feel good about myself. He'd never make me feel like dirt.

Was Forrest that dream guy I always wanted? I wondered. I was a virgin before him. Maybe that's why I loved him so much.

BITTER LOVE

I don't exactly know how our mothers found out. In summer when they did, they were both against us, especially his. "He isn't right for you, Charlene. All he wants is sex," his mother told me.

It would hurt when she'd say those things. At the time I didn't believe her. I started doing everything in the world to get her to love me, but it would not happen.

She sat me down on the front stairs and said, "You're using me to get to my son."

"That's not true."

"Forrest and you are not meant to be," she said, and then she left me to my tears. I was crying so bad that when this nun walked by, she prayed for me. I'm Pentecostal, but that made me feel better. I like church, and I love the Lord.

I felt that Forrest's mother thought I wasn't good

enough for her son. After a while I decided, "I'm going to stop kissing her ass. I'm going on with my life."

Forrest would say, "Let's run away together."

I was tempted. One time I had my purse in my hand and was ready to jump the fence, when my mom came out and caught me.

His sister, Amanda, started lying on me. She told my mother Forrest and I were having oral sex. I didn't even know what that meant until my mother explained it to me.

His other sister hinted Forrest was a dealer.

NO CONTROL

November 16, I come home from school and my mother says, "We're moving."

I'm, like, "Why are people doing this to us?"

I'm upset. I don't want to go. But we're in a shelter. We have no control. All I can think about is Forrest. He's at work. I can't call him.

When he comes home, he says to Bronwyn, "Whose stuff is this out on the porch?"

"Charlene's."

He comes running upstairs. I tell him what happened. The social worker says they're moving us to a motel for a week, then we'll be in another apartment.

I'm crying.

"I guess our love is testing us," I tell him.

We've been together our whole relationship. I've seen him every single day! We don't know what it is to be apart.

REVENGE

After we moved, it was hard to see each other. It was three different bus rides away, and expensive. I never had any money. Forrest would call, and I could hear him putting money in the phone. We'd stay on for hours.

Within a month everything sort of strayed away. I was so lonely and depressed! I fooled around with this guy. I kissed him once, okay?

My relationship with Forrest had been so open, we could talk about anything. When we finally got together, I told him about the kiss. He got mad at me, really mad. He didn't call me for eight days.

I was, "*Ohmigod!*"

To get back at me, Forrest went and did the same thing. And he made sure I found out about it. I felt so low.

Everything was sort of back to normal for three weeks, until one night I called him and he sounded funny. He didn't want to talk right then.

My sister heard he'd just gone wild. Got into trouble with the police. They'd picked him up for dealing. He might go to jail, and it wasn't the first time. She kept saying, "Forrest's no good."

I didn't want to believe her.

I called him back two nights later. Amanda answered and said, "Charlene, Forrest says don't call him no more." Those were her exact words. I'll never forget them.

I exploded. But as soon as I got off the phone, I started crying. I ran past my mother to escape to my bedroom. I couldn't deal with the pain.

It was like somebody dying. That's how I hurt. Day after day, all I did was cry.

I decided, I could not be with somebody like that. A drug dealer. A school dropout. I was at a new school now. I should try to make new friends.

But at the same time, I blamed it all on myself. If Forrest had really been dealing before we moved, I would have known it. Wouldn't I? Could he just have pretended to love me?

I was so confused. I started cursing out everybody that came in my path. I couldn't sleep at night. I'd break out in sweats. "I can't go on like this," I'd tell myself.

Forrest.

Forrest.

Forrest.

I had to get over him.

PILLS AND RAZORS

My mother and I have a relationship that can handle shaky ground. That's how close we are. But she's back east visiting her mother, so I can't really talk to her.

I know I need to talk to someone. I'm so depressed. Everyone I call is out. I even call the mother of my church. She isn't home, either.

I'm, like, I can't take it. I have a semi–nervous breakdown. I'm going to kill myself. It's a spur-of-the-moment thing. I don't write a suicide note.

My mother has high blood pressure and some other medical problems. I find her medication tucked away in her drawer.

I take sleeping pills, pressure pills, phenobarbital. She has them divided into sections—Wednesdays, Thursdays, Fridays. I take whole rows of them.

Then I slash my wrist.

All I remember next is, I pass out and the police are here. My sister has found me. She's so panicky, she's called my aunt.

My aunt says, "What are you calling me for? Call the police."

They take me to the hospital, where they pump my stomach. That's a reason right there not to try suicide. They stick this tube down your nose and, with suction, pull the stuff up from your stomach. It's awful!

I stay three days and two nights. I talk to a psychologist, a brain person. I feel better.

WORTHLESS TEARS

For a month after I got home from the hospital, I never heard from Forrest. I talked to my best friend, Sandra. She's not the kind to go around and spread your business. She's straight.

"It's not worth you crying over this guy," Sandra told me. "If he really did love you as much as he said, he'd have called by now. He knows you're home, and he knows your number."

My mom said, "Let's go to our old church, see some old friends. Maybe that will make you feel better."

We walked in, and Forrest was there! I couldn't look at him. He saw me and smiled.

I started crying, trying to hide it from my mother.

Afterward, I pulled him aside, and he said, "What's up?"

What's up! He had said it like nothing had happened.

"Why did you do it?" I said.

He was, like, "What did I do?"

"You know what you did. You broke up with me over

the phone. You didn't have the decency to tell me your-self. You had your sister tell me."

That's when all hell broke loose. Amanda had made it all up. He never said that. He was screaming at her, "How dare you do something like that!"

Then he said to me, "Charlene, I want you back."

Bronwyn, his other sister, came up and said, "Did you try to kill yourself?"

I was, like, "Yeah. I told the police your brother broke my heart."

Forrest heard that and got angry. He said, "I'm not friends with the police. You shouldn't have mentioned my name to them. Don't ever do that again."

"I'm sorry," I told him.

I couldn't believe it. I was still feeling the pain. He was the one that didn't call me, and there I was saying, "I'm sorry."

SURVIVING LOVE

I've decided to stick to my girlfriends for a while. I might have boyfriends later. I might have sex again. But I'm not going to be sexually active. Not as freaky as those girls having sex every four hours.

Even though Sandra says, "After you've had sex, you

get into it. Your body needs it," I'm trying to hold myself for the right dream guy.

I learned that love's not all about boyfriends and girlfriends. It's about you. You have to care about yourself first. Then if you have to let that person go, it's okay.

You don't have to sit there and try to kill yourself over some guy. You're going to be dead and he's going to be alive, going on with his life, not thinking *twice* about you.

Forrest is now in jail for five months. I don't want to go there to visit him.

THE PRE-SEX INVENTORY

(Suki)

I took God in my life when I was six. Now I'm eighteen. I'm still religious, just not superreligious. I don't like this idea that if you're not Christian, you're going to hell. I pray on my own. I listen to God, not preachers.

God helps me get through at home. My dad's on drugs. My mom's abusive. She sleeps the morning away and then goes shopping for herself and out with the girls.

She hits me and pulls my hair. She says, you stupid this, you lazy that. One day she comes out with the remark, "Suki, you'd make a perfect slut. All you do is lay around."

I don't say what I'm thinking. I can't talk to my mother about anything, let alone sex. I feel like an outcast.

When I was little, my grandmother was my caretaker. She'd help me with my cereal. Walk me to school. I knew my grandmother loved me. Each year for my birthday, she made me these lace dolls.

I turned a lot of my attention to school. I have awards that say I'm motivated. I plan to go to college.

In my neighborhood, your morals are important until you reach a certain age. Then everything changes. I could see how the older girls carry themselves. Most end up having sex by my age.

AFTERNOON RAPE

I met Jeff two years ago, when I was feeling shitty. It was summer, and we'd hang out together. It was nice to get attention.

One afternoon he came over; no one was home. I had my T-shirt on. When he realized I wasn't wearing a bra, he said, "I'm in the mood." He started doing things. He said he wanted to eat me for his Memorial Day picnic.

I was taken by surprise. I told him no. I was a virgin. He said, "Are you sure?" I was insulted.

"I thought you were nice," I said. "I thought you respected me."

He didn't care what I said.

He was pushing me. I was saying, "I don't want to do this. No no no no."

He grabbed me, ripped off my shorts, and started jamming me everywhere. I thought my insides were going to fall out.

I was in such pain. He was making me all swollen. I was bleeding a lot. Afterward, he gave me a rag and said, "Go clean up."

I took it, and as I got off the couch, the trail of blood started following me. When I stopped, it dripped down my leg and pooled on the floor.

I was shaking so much, but still I told him to get out. "You're just using and confusing me," I said. With that, he left.

I went into my bedroom, and I said to myself, "Look what happened. I must be a slut. My life sucks. I don't deserve nice things."

I started to tear up things that meant a lot to me: the lace dolls my grandmother made, the awards from school. I destroyed other stuff in my room. I heard myself say, "I wish I wasn't alive." I picked up a piece of broken glass to cut myself with, but I didn't do it.

Later, I decided I was still a virgin. I was raped, yes. But that has nothing to do with choice or love or sex.

HEALING THE HURT

Now it's two years later. A guy named Robin is in my life. He's talented. He writes for the school newspaper. He wants to work in media arts, directing and writing commercials.

He knows that I go through all sorts of things at home. If I start to go nuts, he grabs my hand. One time Genesis is on *Friday Night Video* playing "No Son of Mine." You see the shadow of the kid. You see the hand and the belt raising. I crack. I start to cry.

Robin figures it out. He explains, "Suki, it's just a video."

"I know," I say, "but I relate to it."

"Your mother doesn't deserve all your thought," he

says. He makes sense. I keep realizing I like hanging out with him. I start flirting with him. He flirts back. But he's shorter than me. And his features aren't exactly what most people call handsome. I'm not ready to admit I'm attracted.

I say, "What would we do if we started dating each other? What's the point?"

He says, "If you have to ask, forget it. The last thing I want to do is add pressure to your life."

"Okay," I say, "let's try it."

The next time I see him, he gives me a quick kiss and a hug. I don't respond. I still think, "It isn't going to work. Why bother?"

But then we keep talking, watching TV, stuff like that.

We talk about kids. For him, no boys, he only wants daddy's little girls to deal with. We wonder, if we had kids, what would they be like?

Of course, I want a gorgeous kid. If the father was Robin, I would want the baby to be a lot like him, too. And as caring as I feel I am.

One day Robin says, "How do you feel about me?"

"I am kind of falling for you."

Then I lean over and give him a full kiss. I say, "I did this? Holy shit! What does this mean?"

"You tell me," he says, meaning I'm the one who initiated it.

I say, "You're not seeing anyone else, are you?"

"No, are you?"

"No."

"Are we exclusive?" he says.

I give him a mile-long smile and say, "I guess it means we're boyfriend and girlfriend." I start to tell him all my secrets.

We also talk about religion. I say, "I'm supposed to be a virgin when I get married."

Robin says, "You're going to listen to a book instead of your emotions? Religion is a crock." I admit that sometimes I battle with religion.

For example, marriages are supposed to be blessed. Well, if they are, how come there's so much divorce? Maybe if you respect the person you're with, if you totally love him, it's okay to have sex if you're planning to stay together.

I think about getting married. I'll find a nice dress, not a wedding dress. And it can be whatever color I choose.

It depends on what mood I'm in; it might be something subtle or off-the-shoulder, with a piece of jewelry. I want flowers in my hair, and I'll wear it up.

I'd be very selective who would come. Robin's family, even though his mother left when he was four and just came back into his life this year.

He let her know, "You may be my mother, but don't tell me what to do." I'd invite my grandmother. I don't know about my parents.

NO PIECE OF MEAT

Robin doesn't feel that sex outside of marriage is a sin. He says, "I respect your beliefs, but they're bullshit." Sometimes I agree with him. Other times I don't know. To me it's important to be a virgin.

Still, part of me wants to have sex.

I think, "It would be great to have parents to talk to about sexual feelings." But I don't. I decide, though, I shouldn't ask a friend who's sexually active for advice. She'd tell me, "Yeah, do it."

I should try to talk to an adult. Then it's still up to me to decide whether that person makes sense. To get started, to help me think, I make an inventory.

This way I won't get caught unable to explain myself to Robin, or any guy, who pressures me. I don't want to say yes to something I don't want. I don't want to ever be in a situation again like I was with Jeff.

Here's what I write.

[1.] It will only give me heartache if I have sex just because:
  • Robin asks me
  • I want to prove my love
  • I feel like less of a person if I don't

Then I go on to my next part. I imagine why Robin wants to sleep with me. I add to my checklist.

[2.] Robin wants to have sex because:
- he loves me
- I'm physically attractive
- he's horny

[3.] Where does he want to do it?
- a parked car
- his house
- a motel
- my house

[4.] What problems can happen?
- sexually transmitted diseases
- the condom breaks
- it will hurt because I'm totally nervous
- pregnancy!

I think about what would happen if my parents found out. How would they react? How would Robin's dad react? What would I do if I got pregnant? I feel if I'm not ready for the responsibility of a baby, I shouldn't have sex. And I shouldn't have sex unless I'm going to be protected.

I know some girls sleep with a guy and do certain things that the guy wants when they don't really want to. If I'm not sure whether I want to do something, I shouldn't let Robin talk me into it.

I also know girls who have sex because they've had

sex before with another guy. They're a piece of meat for the latest one to dine on. I don't want to be like that.

If I'm not ready for sex, I shouldn't do it.

I can't forget AIDS. Even though I think I know everything about him, maybe I don't. I should find out as much as I can. If I compromise, sleep with Robin, and then decide that I made a mistake, I'll tell him, "Let's take a step back and not have sex again."

If he says no, then he's not worth it. And he shouldn't be questioning me as to why, unless he's doing it in an inquisitive way and not in a hey-we-already-did-it, it-doesn't-matter-anymore way.

LOVE TRUST

It's eleven months that Robin and I have been together. We do things that are physical but not quite sexual. Like, he'll kiss me and rub my stomach.

One time he stopped touching my body. He went downstairs and got some sodas. When he came back up, I said, "What's wrong?"

He said, "I know you're not ready to go further. I was getting excited. I didn't want anything to happen that shouldn't happen."

Now, though, he feels I don't trust him as much as I should. He's proven himself, which is true.

He says, "I'm not pressuring you, but can't you be more relaxed and uninhibited?"

At first I wouldn't even close my eyes. He says, "Closing your eyes helps you block things out." Now I do it for a couple seconds at a time.

Still he knows I hold back. He wants me to take the initiative, do as I feel, not wait for him to make the moves. I try that, and it sort of works.

I can give the first kiss, but I won't stick my tongue in his mouth or anything like that. I'd rather let him put his tongue in mine and then respond to him.

ONE HUNDRED PERCENT SURE

Robin lets me know that while he'll wait for me, he doesn't have to like it. He wishes we could make love. "Organized religion," he says, "is a way of controlling society."

"Maybe yes, maybe no," I tell him. "But I'm the one who has to control my sexual feelings, my body, and my life. I've prayed to God about it. For now, I still want to be more than one hundred percent sure before I give up my virginity."

F✦ACT B✦OX

Girl Scouts Survey on the Beliefs and Moral Values of America's Children

You have had a steady relationship for a long time and you feel very much in love. At this point your girlfriend or boyfriend tells you they want to have sex with you. In this situation, you would probably . . .

	HAVE SEX	TRY TO HOLD OFF	REFUSE FOR NOW	WAIT UNTIL MARRIAGE
Total:	37%	19%	19%	24%
Junior high:	27%	20%	22%	31%
Senior high:	47%	19%	17%	17%
Male:	54%	11%	17%	17%
Female:	22%	22%	26%	30%

—Girl Scouts of the USA, 830 Third Avenue, New York, NY 10022. *Fieldwork:* Fall 1989.

CONTROLLING THE MONSTER

(Elizabeth)

"Let's go to Lucy's to watch the fireworks," says Andrew.

The Fourth of July is my favorite holiday, and he knows it.

"Great," I say.

Andrew and I have been sort of together for nearly a year. He's hard as hell. Exciting. Sexually mature. He's also brilliant. All the girls are after him.

I make up conversations in my head where I tell him, "I'm going to really get you someday. You'll be head over heels in love with me. We'll have a forever connection, a place of our own. We can rent movies, order take-out, and just sit around."

Instead, he breaks my heart so many times.

It's hot out that day. Andrew takes off his shirt and is strutting through the crowd feet ahead of me.

I'm, like, "Helloooo."

He yells back at me, "I need a beer," and disappears into a bar. Within minutes he's drinking pitchers by himself.

"You show no concern for me," I say.

"So what? Other times I'm all over you." And with that he starts feeling me up in front of a bar full of people. I'm embarrassed and angry. I push him away.

"I'm going to Lucy's party," he says. "Take it or leave it."

"You're on your own," I say, and storm out the door.

There I am walking the streets, feeling alone. This

always seems to happen. I'm, like, "I'm leaving him for good. This is it!"

But where am I going to go? Not home, for sure. That's boring. I love my parents, but they're caught up in their own lives. My older brother, Mr. Perfect, doesn't have time for me, either.

When Andrew first really hassled me, I told my parents about it. My dad went over to his house and yelled at him. He said, "That's my daughter, and I love her. How could you hurt her?"

It shook Andrew up. He respects my dad. I thought, "Andrew's so upset, maybe now if we get back together, the screaming will be over." And it was, for a while.

THE ULTIMATE CRIME

I start missing Andrew. I figure I'll go to Lucy's and find him.

By the time I get to her house, the party's taken over. I go upstairs and knock on a couple doors. Nobody answers. I walk into a bedroom.

"Andrew!"

He's with this girl Marilyn. She's fully clothed, and he's in his boxers. She's straddling him. I'm devastated. The ultimate crime in front of my eyes.

"Get the hell out of here!" he screams at me.

"I hate you, Andrew! You, too, Marilyn," I say while I'm crying and running down the stairs. "And Marilyn, I don't want to hate you, because before this I liked you."

"You bitch!" Andrew yells after me. "Where do you get off causing me problems? You bring out the worst in me." Next thing I know, he's chasing me. Half-dressed. We're out on the streets screaming at each other, until people we don't know threaten to call the police.

Andrew's scary when he's drunk. But I kind of find it —not exciting, but sort of like an adventure in a way. We're both these crazy rebels.

"We need to discuss what's going on," I tell him.

"We know what's going on. Marilyn makes me feel good. If you showed me more affection, I wouldn't get upset and turn to others."

"But sometimes I just want to hang out with you," I say. "I don't want to have sex."

"Sex means love," he says.

That stops me. Confuses me. "Maybe you're right, Andrew. I know you always tell me how your parents deprived you of love and attention when you were little."

"Yeah," he says, "and you're just doing more of the same."

He starts to croon, "Oh, sweetie, I'm so lucky. I can't believe I have you in my life." He yells at me, and then he wants to hold me, treat me like a baby.

Finally he says, "I swear to God, I'll never scream at you again."

The next day, when Andrew's sober, I ask him, "What is going through your mind when you're treating me like that?"

He only focuses on the screaming, not on any reasons behind it. He says, "You don't think when you're screaming at someone. You don't plan it."

"So how do you know you're not going to do it again?"

"I just won't."

I tell him that if the screaming just comes, it's like a monster that takes him over. "It's the same as being high. And I don't think any guy can say 'I'll never do it again' without some kind of help. You're not in control of it. It's controlling you."

"The only thing that's controlling me is you," he says, as he picks up my address book. He crosses out names and starts totally ripping it up.

"Now I have a little control back over you," he says. "Those people are out of your life." In case I miss his point, he holds an umbrella at my neck. Then he laughs.

I'm in shock.

His mom comes into the room, and I say, "Your son has problems that need to be resolved." She's, like, from outer space. All she says is, "Don't go blaming your problems on my Andrew."

"Forget it," I say. "We're over."

"You'll be back," he says, when I walk out the door for the zillionth time.

THE COMMITMENT

This time is different. I go out with a guy named Hank. He goes to another school. Hank keeps saying, "Elizabeth, you're wonderful. You're beautiful."

"What fun," I think.

When Andrew hears I'm seeing somebody, *he's* shocked. I've always been accessible to him. He has me no matter what. After I tell him, "Hank gave me my first orgasm ever," overnight he changes.

Andrew gets obsessed with me.

He shows up at our back door, drunk, demanding a commitment.

"Me being committed to you and you not being committed to me?" I say. "Is that what you mean? What about all those girls?"

"They were just revenge. You and me, we're meant for each other."

He hasn't said "I love you," but he's close to it.

"I want to share something with you. I want you to have my baby," he says.

I'm thinking, "Come on, Andrew, say it, say it, tell me you love me."

"I lub you, Elizabeth."

Yes! I got him to say it!

NO-WIN SITUATION

I decide to really pay attention to the things that upset Andrew. If I see what I do to trigger a bad response in him, I can stop doing it. Our problems will be over.

One Sunday we're at my house. My parents are gone for the weekend. He says, "Make a couple sandwiches." I go into the kitchen, make two, and bring them back to my room.

The screaming starts. "There's too much fat and not enough calories in them!" I'm supposed to remember he's body-building.

I'm wearing this ballerina pin my mom and dad gave me the Christmas I turned five. It seems to symbolize when I was younger and felt safe.

Andrew tears the pin off my shirt and smashes it with his fist. I spit on him. He punches me in the arm.

Right then, my mom calls to see how I am. "Oh, fine," I say.

After I hang up, I think, "If I'm ever a mother, I don't want my daughter to say she's fine when she's in danger." There are times I'm in a corner crying, I picture being in my parents' arms.

By now, they hate him. They know I'd only sneak if they forbid me from seeing him. They'd like to, though.

I feel I'm a burden to them. All we talk about is Andrew.

A PASSIVE LIFE

Before Andrew, I collected a lot of friends. They labeled me confident. I pictured myself as leading the crowd, making others feel at ease.

Now I only socialize with him and his friends. They don't see him as a brute and me as a victim. They think, "Elizabeth's a bitch. She agitates Andrew. How could anyone put up with her?"

Is there something wrong with me? Do I have a temper, like Andrew says?

I feel he's isolated me. When I'm not with him, I live in this little planet, my room. I keep my shades down. When I talk, I stumble over words. I'm not sure of myself. I'm not a leader. I'm not a follower.

I'm a passive.

How can I leave him? I'd be too lonely. If I got together with one of my old friends, what would we do? Go to the movies? Anyway, the whole time I'd wish I was with Andrew.

I want to be with him because it's what I want to do.

I don't have anywhere to go if I'm not with him.

I love him.

And supposedly he loves me.

I try to break up, and he calls, begging me and begging me. Crying. He says, "I'm going crazy without you."

I tell him not to call. The phone rings, and it's such a part of my life, even though I know I shouldn't answer it, I don't want to, I pick it up. Then it's impossible for me to hang up on him.

Sure, maybe he's extremely selfish. But people in general are selfish. They're into themselves. Andrew pays a lot of attention to me, and I can't get past that situation.

Still, there are more instances where I tell people, "Oh, yeah, we had this violent fight." I'm embarrassed. But I also want people to know so they can tell me, *"This is abuse."*

I don't want to have to figure it out myself.

Andrew doesn't hit me in the face. He doesn't slap me. He leaves no bruises to see. I never end up in the hospital. We yell at each other. He destroys things of mine that matter. How can it be abuse?

Can it?

I tell him, "I'm going to see a therapist."

"I'll be your therapist," he says.

The person who's causing the problem is the only one I can talk to about it. It's insane.

ATTENTION STARVED

I call a hotline. I get a number for a counselor, who runs a group for teen girls in abusive relationships. I show up at a meeting.

"You're attention starved," one of the girls says.

"And Andrew's abuse is attention," says another.

"You're asking your mom and dad to get involved in this drama," the counselor says.

I don't like the way they all gang up on me. They don't understand me. I come from a more sophisticated background than they do.

They say it's about old stuff, too. Like my feelings about having famous parents, or times when my dad would be drunk and yell at me.

"I won't see Andrew anymore," I say. But that's to get them off my case.

F✲CT B✲X

Surviving Abuse Like Hostages Do

The baffling problem of why abused women often remain in harmful relationships is undergoing a new appraisal by some mental health experts. They now say these women exhibit a behavior that can develop in classic hostage situations. . . .

Among abused women, often the victim is grateful for any act of kindness the abuser shows her, denies the abuse, is hypervigilant to the abuser's needs, finds it difficult to leave the abuser and fears the abuser will come back to get her if she ends the relationship.

She sees this person as her only friend. This is also a person who has given her life. This is the only identity she has now.

These feelings might be even more likely to develop in young women's dating relationships, experts say. One reason is that young women are more likely to perceive violence as evidence of love.

—*Los Angeles Times*, August 26, 1991

HEARTBREAK ON VALENTINE'S DAY

(Yvelyne)

128

132

THINGS THAT
MAKE US CRY

(Eric)

S ometimes I worried, "Am I crazy?" I was fifteen and had actually never even *kissed* a girl. I was definitely interested in changing that. Her name was Michelle.

Six of us, including Michelle, were on a bus going to an environmental conference. My idea was to wait until the end to ask her out. That way, if she said no, I wouldn't have to feel stupid for the whole rest of the trip.

There I was, getting my confidence together, when this girl Liza calls out across a couple rows of seats, "Hey, Eric! You want to go to the Thanksgiving Dance?"

Liza came with rumors and a reputation: a brilliant crazy who went around with weird people. I looked at Michelle, trying to make an expression that said, I don't want to. But then I looked back at Liza and thought, "Maybe it'll be fun."

"Okay," I said.

GRAVEYARD CONTRACT

About our third time out, Liza and I got drunk in the graveyard and talked about things that made us cry.

She told me that about a month earlier, she'd been raped by this guy she'd just met at the mall. "It's changed me," she said. "I don't want to ever have sex again."

I felt sorry for her and lost interest in Michelle.

I said to Liza, "I'll prove to you there are good people in the world."

We talked about our families. Her parents were always on her case. Even though my parents were divorced, they taught me morals: Help those who need help. Don't take more than my share of the pie. That sort of thing.

"It's hard to stick to your beliefs," Liza said.

She was right. We go to a traditional Alabama high school. Football is a big part of life. Homecoming and prom are important, too. But not for me. I volunteer for Greenpeace. I ran for class president on a platform of political issues.

"Do you think I'm crazy?" I asked her.

"No," she said. "You're just different from other guys. You're gentle, respectful." Then she confessed she thought I must not like her much. I didn't make any advances.

"Sure, I like you. I'm just shy." I didn't want her to know I was inexperienced.

Liza talked about her grades. They were outstanding. "But they're my only identification. Maybe now," she teased me, "I'll be known as 'Eric's girlfriend.' "

This whole time we'd been drinking. She told me she was the addictive type. She started to cry. "I wonder what it would be like if we both stopped drinking? For good," she said.

"Maybe we'd be able to deal with our feelings better," I said. "Why don't we sign a contract that we won't drink or use drugs?"

"Only if we seal it with a kiss," she said.

We did, and everything seemed exciting and optimistic. Every hour with her was different. Her moods seemed to blow with the wind. Mine don't change in the same way.

AFTERNOON LOVE

By Christmas, I'm walking her to class. Holding hands with her in the halls.

Sometimes we visit historic houses in town. We take photographs of each other with them in the background. We like to talk about politics, religion, and world peace. When we're alone, we also have what Liza calls "kissing lessons." It's an excuse not to be embarrassed.

After that, I guess you can say we get more serious. I want to have sex, but I'm not going to even mention it. It's up to her.

We're spending more and more time in my room. When my mom's home, she's upstairs in her half of the house. Liza and I come and go, and she doesn't really notice. Mom's a modest person, too; she understands. She never comes in my room uninvited.

One afternoon over the vacation, Liza says, "You know, Eric, if we make love, I'd consider it a recovery. I've regained confidence in males."

She started on the Pill.

CRAZY LOVE

On a Thursday evening in January, Liza's mother finds the birth control pills. "You and Eric aren't going to see each other anymore," she announces.

Liza calls me right away. "I don't know how I can go on without you."

I get pretty emotional, too.

She says, "I'll call right back. I need to get some water. Don't do anything." I'm sitting there, not knowing what's really going on.

When she finally does call, she says her mom agreed we can get together, but with these rules:

We can only see each other once a week.

We are only allowed to be together if we are with other teenagers or a parent is watching us.

We can never go into each other's bedroom ever again.

"I don't see any way out of these rules," Liza tells me.

The next time I call, her brother tells me, "She's in the hospital. She swallowed all these pills." I'm shocked.

I sneak into the hospital, up to intensive care, and stay with her a couple hours. Three days later, I break the contract and start drinking again.

I feel Liza tried to end her life because of our love, and I didn't. During school I swallow forty-eight of the same pills she has. I'm not going to tell anybody. I'll just go home, go to sleep, and never wake up.

But all of a sudden, in between classes, there's Liza! She is back in school talking about recovery. I don't know what to do. I shouldn't have, but I tell Liza what I've done.

Before she goes to her scheduled therapist appointment, she tells her mom what I did. By the time I get home, both of them are there. They take me to the emergency room. To make sure I go, they call my mom and the police, too.

At the hospital Liza asks the doctor, "Can I come in now to see Eric?"

"You've caused him enough trouble already," he tells her. She starts *shrieking*, running up and down the halls at the hospital.

They take her to the top floor and commit her for depression. The next thing I know, they're taking me to another hospital. They say, "We don't want you at the same hospital."

I felt like I was caged in. "You don't have any real problems," they kept telling me. "You only went along with it. You copied Liza."

It was awful. In order to get out as soon as I could, I had to agree with what they said. Two weeks later, they let me go. Within a week Liza was out, too.

We'd been planning to go to the Valentine Dance. "What about that?" I asked her.

"Oh, I'm going with Patrick."

"Break the date."

"No," she said. "Eric, if you want to know the truth, I lost faith in you when you tried to commit suicide. I wanted you there to support me. You were supposed to be the stable one."

"What?"

"Everybody's pressuring me not to see you for a while. They blame you for the trouble we got in," she said.

"What!" I finally said.

"I lost a lot of trust in you. You lied to me. You told *me* not to 'do anything,' then you tried to kill yourself."

I felt terrible. I didn't like that she was telling everybody what had happened. I wasn't telling anyone. I wanted to keep it a secret.

I escaped into sleep. My mom didn't press me much. She blamed Liza and didn't want us to be together anymore. She said, "There're better people in the world for you."

I was determined, though, to get Liza back. I called her, saying we had to talk.

She said, "No, and anyway, I don't think you're really capable of opening up to me."

That made me more upset. My mom told me that most men can't talk about their feelings. She wanted me to be able to.

She taught me through examples. In a movie she'd point out when a male was angry, instead of talking about his feelings, he, like, jumped in his car and raced away. My mom would say, "Eric, it's better to face your emotions than run away."

FULL CIRCLE

Before all this, my mom and I talked a lot. After my breakup, I stopped talking to her.

I went out and didn't come home. Sometimes I stayed out all night. I started drinking and doing drugs more and more.

I missed Liza, even though I felt *relieved* without her. To get back my old life, I decided to have a party. I invited Liza, too. About forty people showed up, including her. She came with a girlfriend, but the girlfriend left.

Liza stayed and said, "Do you want me to hang around and help you clean up?"

Things grew from there. Liza said, "Let's agree not to make any more promises, and seal it with a kiss." We did.

About two weeks later we went to see the movie *The Cutting Edge*. Liza was driving. In the car going home I criticized the personality of the main female character: "She was selfish, materialistic, and treated men badly. She held power over them. That was the way she liked to deal with them."

Everything I said bad about the character, Liza took personally. I tried to explain to her that it was the movie, not her.

She didn't understand. She didn't care. She got all worked up.

She stops the car and tells me to get out.

I get out and walk home. That's the end of the relationship for me. The next day I pick up the phone and call Michelle.

Michelle answers. I say, "There's an Earth Day planning session. I wondered if you wanted to come along?"

"Okay," she says. "It'll give us a chance to get to know each other better."

A GENTLEMAN OR A WUSS?

(Amy)

The other night at the bowling alley a certain individual told my best friend, Vickie, I was a slut. She punched him in the mouth and said, "That's just a taste of what you're going to get if I ever hear you say that about Amy again."

See, before this year I had a bad reputation. What people don't know is, I was raped so many times, it took me, I'd say, months just to be able to kiss a guy again.

After that I went a little crazy, I guess. I started sneaking out a lot. I slept around.

Now my reputation has changed. It's: Amy's all right. She's understanding. You can talk to her and not have her open up her big mouth.

The difference is Waylon.

It started the very beginning of the year in ROTC, when I was still going out with Frankie. I was catching a ride home, and Waylon was massaging my shoulder and holding my hand in the backseat.

I'm, like, "What am I getting myself into?"

About a week later, me and Frankie break up. I'm in tears over at my best friend Vickie's house. Vickie and Waylon have been good friends this last year. She waits until I leave the room and calls him.

She goes, "Guess what, Waylon. I've got some news."

He goes, "What?"

"Well, you know Amy?"

"Yeah. What about her?"

"Her and her boyfriend just broke up."

He goes, "*Really?* That's great! I mean—well, you know what I mean."

Vickie goes, "Yeah, I know what you mean."

"Is she there?"

"Yeah."

So I get on the phone. We arrange it so we do a ROTC color-guard practice the next day.

Well, we do our practice, and afterward Waylon has his arms around my waist. Everything is perfect until Frankie walks in and gets ticked.

I say, "Waylon, stop. There's my ex."

He's going, "Oh, yeah? Watch this." And he kisses me. Frankie starts punching the wall and stuff, and then he leaves.

All of a sudden an argument breaks out. I'm the type of person, if someone messes with my friends, they mess with me. So I leave Waylon's side, and I start getting in a fight with this guy.

Waylon goes, "Amy, sit down. I don't feel like getting in a fight, and if he slaps you, I'm going to have to kick his butt."

I say, "Waylon, I'm a big girl. I can take care of myself."

Waylon is dragging me off, and I'm still yelling at this other guy. Waylon goes, "Amy."

I go, "What?"

"Do you want to go out with me?"

I say, "Yes," and I keep yelling. Then I say, "Wait a minute. What did you say?"

"I asked you out."

"And I said 'yes'?"

"Yes."

"Okay."

I just totally forget about the fight.

SECURELY VULNERABLE

When me and Waylon were going out, he said what he liked best about me was my personality. I could open up and tell him anything that I was feeling without making him uncomfortable.

He liked my eyes. They change color with the season. He said he thought I was pretty. Not only on the outside but on the inside, too.

What attracted me to Waylon was his sincerity, his courtesy, and he certainly was a gentleman. He didn't burp at the table or backwash his soda. He stuck out from the crowd. He was a guy that's secure but at times vulnerable.

That's because of the way he was raised, because of his daddy. He died in battle for the United States. That's how Waylon wants to die, serving his country. When he told me that story, it made me look at him with different eyes. I'm loyal to the U.S., too.

What finally did it, though, was the way Waylon made me feel. No matter how down I was—this is when we were friends—he could make me smile. He was there for me. He was tender and protective.

What he couldn't do, though, that really matters is tell me what I need to hear. That he cares about me. He needs me. I make him feel he's needed.

FALLING TOO FAST

We went out for a month and two weeks and broke up first at the military ball. He felt he was falling for me too fast.

I'm seventeen and he's sixteen. He'd had one other serious girlfriend. He didn't realize he loved her until they broke up. I think he was thinking, "Amy's on my mind all the time. Maybe I'm in love with her."

But he never told me he loved me.

He admits it to other people but not me. Vickie says, "Waylon just can't look you in the eye and say, 'Amy, I love you.'"

"Why not?" I say.

"I think he's afraid you'd laugh at him. You'd say, 'What? Are you nuts?' "

I guess unless you get a wham-bam-thank-you-ma'am kind, that's normal for most guys at sixteen.

LOVE SONG

A couple days after we broke up, Waylon was over. There's nobody home but the two of us. I put on the Bonnie Raitt song "I Can't Make You Love Me."

I say, "I want you to listen to the song," and I start singing it to him.

He says, "Don't."

I keep singing, and then at the end I say to him, "I love you."

He looks at me and says, "This is incredible. You break up with me, but take a piece of me with you. I want it back!"

"How could I give it back?"

He goes, "Then no matter where you go, I want you to keep it with you."

THE EXPLOSIVE LETTER

That was the closest he came to opening up to me. Two days later, I find out that he's mad again because of something I supposedly said that I didn't say. See, there was a girl trying to break us up.

I wanted to stop this whole thing before it exploded. I walk up to him and say, "Waylon, we've got to talk. When's a good time that you're off from work?"

This was Monday. He says, "I'll be off Wednesday."

I don't want to keep this inside me that long, but what can I do?

"All right," I say. "Where should we meet?"

He says, "I'll see you at the mall Wednesday."

Wednesday comes along. I say to him, "Waylon, are we meeting this afternoon?"

"No way," he says. "I'm going home, and I'm going to sleep."

I say, "Waylon, this is *important*."

He goes, "Well, it's just going to have to wait."

"But it can't wait."

"It's going to have to."

I say, "Fine," and walk off.

When I have basic problems, I'm closest to my mother. When I have a problem mainly with a guy, I end up with my father. He's a male.

I tell my daddy what happened. He says, "Waylon's

not a gentleman. He's a wuss. He never should have left you hanging."

I go into my room, sit down, and write down every-thing I feel: Waylon is acting like a jerk. Waylon can't tell a girl what she needs to hear.

Then I give this letter to Brian, practically my male best friend, to see what he thinks. He reads it and starts thinking, "If I give this to Waylon, maybe it'll get him and Amy talking."

Of course, I don't know this. I go to class, and during their lunch block Brian walks up to Waylon and says, "Here, you better read this."

Waylon says, "What is it?"

Brian says, "Something Amy wrote. Brace yourself. You're not going to like what you read."

Waylon reads it and gets really ticked. He walks by my door and stops.

We have eye contact for, like, five minutes. We never did that before. Right then, I know something is up. I whisper to Vickie about the letter, and she says, "You just messed up bad. You're wrong about Waylon."

THE FEELINGS INSIDE

I got home and called Waylon to try to fix things. Well, he would not talk to me. Period. By the time I was on the bus the next day, you can imagine how I felt.

Joey, his best friend that lives right down the road from me, says, "If I were you, I wouldn't go nowhere near Waylon."

"Why?"

"He doesn't want to see your face. He cannot stand you!"

My voice cracks.

Joey goes, "Why'd you write that letter?"

I start crying. "Joey, you know I'm not that type of person to keep my feelings inside."

"At least you could have waited awhile."

"I couldn't. It was eating at me."

He goes, "You just lost his friendship and anything else y'all could have had."

Once I got into school, I walked up to Waylon. He just rolled his eyes, walked the other way, and over his shoulder yelled, "Bitch." My heart went flip-flop.

I went into the ROTC room, put down my books, went back into the hall to walk by Waylon. He barked at me. The only time Waylon ever barked was when he saw an ugly girl. He goes, "Oof, give that skank some Kibble & Bits, and she'll be good to go."

I was the only girl around. I started crying again. He

didn't know, because I didn't start until I was past him. All my friends came around me and said, "Give up on him, Amy."

I yelled at them, "I don't want anybody else. All I want is Waylon!"

I finally decided the best way for me to take care of my situation was to get enough guts to talk to Waylon. During lunch I walked up to him. My eyes were all red and puffy from crying for three periods.

I said, "Waylon, can I talk to you?"

He said, "I don't have nothing to say to you."

I said, "I just want you to listen to me."

"You have five minutes. By that time I should be done with my cigarette, and I'll be back inside the school building."

I said, "I got all your messages." All his messages were that he didn't want me to call him. He didn't want no letters, no nothing from me.

I said, "I know an apology won't help, but you don't know how sorry I am."

He said, "We did have a chance, but you shot that to hell and back."

That was like a knife going through me. I said, "I don't care what you say to me. I don't care what you do to me. I don't care what you say about me, whether it's in my face or behind my back. I'll *always* love you."

He said, "I don't know how much that weighs anymore," and he walked away. Just like that.

I cried some more. A whole week went by. We were totally ignoring each other. I called Vickie to tell her the latest. She said she was going to the mall. Meet her there. I showed up, and Waylon—just to bug me 'cause he knew I was there all the time—he started flirting with Vickie, my best friend!

You know how much that hurt me? She was pushing him away, saying, "How are you and Amy doing?" She already knew, but she wanted to hear his side of the story. I walked back out. I couldn't take it.

She told me he started calling me a bunch of bad names, pardon my French. She jumped on him and said, "I'm sorry, but all you got out of that letter was what you wanted to get from it.

"You didn't get the pure meaning behind it. Amy was telling you that you need to open up. You didn't tell her nothing about how you were feeling. Don't go blaming this all on her."

"The least she could have done was told me," Waylon said.

She went, "Waylon, if you remember, Amy tried to tell you. She told you to meet her, and what did you say? You wanted to go home and sleep." And she emphasized the word *sleep*.

"I didn't look at it that way."

She said, "Maybe you should have," and she walked off.

Waylon was following her all around the mall. All

my friends were cutting him down low, saying, "Look at that dweeb."

THE DOUBLE APOLOGY

The next day, I walk into school for the ROTC banquet. Waylon is watching me and watching me. I turn around and say, "You've put me through enough of this pain. Why more?"

He turns away and ignores me the rest of the night.

The very next day, he's going, "Amy, Amy." Now I'm ignoring him. Finally, though, I turn around and say, "I thought you weren't talking to me."

He goes, "Well, I wasn't."

"What do you want, then?"

"I'm going to tell you something that might get me in trouble, but I want to tell you anyway."

"What?"

It was something about ROTC and I might be getting a promotion.

I go, "Waylon."

"What?"

We're still walking side by side down the hallway in silence. I go, "I'm sorry."

"For what?"

"You know, the letter and everything. Am I forgiven?"

"It all depends."

"On what?"

"If you forgive me," he says.

"What for?"

" 'Cause I kind of acted like a prick."

I say, "Yeah, you did. But that's beside the point. I deserved it."

"Yeah, but you didn't deserve it that bad."

Then I say, "Friends?"

He goes, "Yeah."

I get a big smile on my face. He says, "Amy, can I have a hug?"

I melt and give him a hug.

F𝒜CT B·O·X

Before or After Saying "I Do"

Living happily ever after is less a mystery than the mastery of certain skills, modern researchers say. They have devised a 125-point test to tell if a relationship will last. For a brief example, agree or disagree with these statements:

- I find it very easy to share my private feelings with my partner.
- I feel good about how we make decisions and settle arguments.
- Love is not a sufficient condition for a happy marriage.
- I think it is best if a couple equally shares household chores.

The more yeses the better; but also the more two mates' answers agree, the better.
—*The New York Times*, August 16, 1992

If you have a love story you would like to
share for a future book, please write us:

Bode/Mack
c/o Delacorte Press
1540 Broadway
New York, New York 10036

WITH THANKS

Many thanks to our families and friends: Barbara and Carolyn Bode; Pearl, Kenny, and Peter Mack; Lucy Cefalu, Richard Eagan, Kay Franey, Harriet and Ted Gottfried, Carole Mayedo, Marvin Mazor, Michael Sexton, and the Third Thursday Writers Group.

The following people also provided us with invaluable assistance: Linda Arce, media specialist, Hamilton Fish Library, New York, New York; Donna Armstrong, media specialist, Elkton Middle School, Elkton, Maryland; Chris Austen and Donna Chumas, media specialists, Patchogue-Medford High School, Patchogue, New York; Fred Bayer, media specialist, South Ocean Middle School, Patchogue, New York; Doris Fleischer, Cardozo High School, Bayside, New York; Jane Jury, media specialist, Elkton High School, Elkton, Maryland; Karen Land, media specialist, Greenport Public School, Greenport, New York; Linda Maggio, assistant director, Mount Sinai Pediatric School Health Project, New York, New York; Arlene Morales-Weber, media specialist, Marine Park Intermediate School, Sheepshead Bay, New York; Tally Negroni, media specialist, Stamford High School, Stamford, Connecticut; Jolie Truman, Oregon Middle School, Medford, New York; Susan Viola, media specialist, Shelter Island UFSD, Shelter Island, New York.

And of course, a special thank you to the individual teenagers who volunteered to share their stories. If they hadn't been willing to open their lives, this book would not exist.

JANET BODE writes hard-hitting nonfiction books for and about teen-agers. Through group discussions and one-on-one interviews, she uncovers the personal stories behind today's headlines, then reports them to her readers. Several of her books, including *The Voices of Rape: Healing the Hurt*, *New Kids on the Block: Oral Histories of Immigrant Teens*, and *Beating the Odds: Stories of Unexpected Achievers*, have been selected Best Books for Young Adults. Her book *Different Worlds: Interracial and Cross-Cultural Dating* was made into a CBS-TV schoolbreak special. *Heartbreak and Roses* is her tenth YA title.

STAN MACK is a reporter/cartoonist whose comic strip appears in *The Village Voice*, the weekly newspaper of New York City. In addition to creating graphic nonfiction stories for Bode's books, he's at work on a series of humorous adult history books. He also did a comic strip called "Out-Takes" for *Adweek*, a national advertising maga-zine, and is the author/illustrator of *Ten Bears in My Bed*, a popular children's picture book.